CAELESTI

SUMUS

OMNES

SEMINE

ORIUNDI

YOUR LOWLY HEDGEHOG KNOWS

Also by Gareth Howell-Jones

Do Not Call the Tortoise

"Stunning – full of revelatory beauty." (*Katherine May*)

"Wonderful, funny & profound." (*Jay Griffiths*)

"Imagine a 21st century Rubaiyat of Omar Khayyam, drenched in Wordsworth and laced with Darwin. That's something but only something – of this vital, prescient, kind and companionable book... Here is the wisdom of the hedgerow and the mountain; the power of entanglement; the electricity of encounter. Marvellous and marvellously important." (*Charles Foster*)

"I am a great believer in STA. It has enriched my life deeply." (*Max Porter*)

"Beautiful and singular" (*Horatio Clare*)

"A shrine to thoughtfulness & the rich, neglected virtues of reflection." (*Adam Nicolson*)

'A hugely readable, empathetic and ingenious braiding of philosophy, poetry, art and history brought together with a love for the natural world to show how we might yet exist alongside it more fully.' (*Owen Sheers*)

YOUR
LOWLY
HEDGEHOG
KNOWS

Gareth Howell-Jones

THE CYRUS PRESS

CONTENTS

Preface	11
The Gigantic Drama	13
In Search of Self-Evident Truths	17
Mr Bun and the Leaves and Flowers	27
Raising Ghosts	35
Lichen	45
Unified Lives	47
The Inscrutability of Woodlice	55
Phlo Flow	61
Not Mrs Tiggywinkle	71
Bacon & Keats	79
Life is Creativity	85

There's a small knot of people, one with a clipboard, some in hi-viz, gathered beneath the huge old tree by the castle wall. What are they thinking as they gaze up into its branches?

It's a beech or, as clipboard-man might say, a Fagus sylvatica. They might be saying it's beautiful, even noble – I'd agree – or that it's a nuisance and 'needs to come down'. Perhaps some see it as a biodiversity habitat or valuable carbon sink, an important landscape feature, a source of fine timber, or even firewood. But the thing itself towers above our thoughts of how it might be useful to us, how to classify it. The thing itself isn't even a tree – 'tree' is just a word we have invented to tell ourselves it's not a shrub. All we can honestly and impartially say is that it is itself, a unique living organism. As are we all. It knows and cares nothing about the man who says he owns it, nor the words we use to pin it down.

This book is an attempt to communicate in words, so I'll carry on writing 'tree', and you'll carry on understanding what I mean, but it's worth cherishing somewhere in our hearts the deep unknowability of that beech, of each of the people gathered at its foot and, of course, of ourselves.

> *Not knowing*
> *The name of the tree*
> *I stood in the flood*
> *Of its sweet smell*
>
> *Bashō (trans. Nobuyuki Yuasa)*

PREFACE

Creativity flows through every living thing, so writing a book needs no apology. Asking anyone to read it is a different matter, however – there are so many other things to do. But the way of looking at the world I've stumbled across, more by chance than cleverness, is so rewarding, so reassuring, so simple and obvious, yet so profound in its effects that I've felt compelled to share it. Of course, it isn't my invention; this is just a new take on an old way of living which your lowly hedgehog, for one, already knows. That it is so divergent from the social-political-media narrative we absorb each day is a shock. Given the continuing failure of that system, perhaps it is also an opportunity.

The title is taken from the Jake Thackray song, *Remember Bethlehem*, a beautiful lyric from someone better known for his satire. In telling the Nativity story he claims that the whole of nature – hills, nightingales, his own flesh and blood, pussy-willows, fish and daffodils – understands what's going on. *Your lowly hedgehog knows what it means*. If there is a god, it must be a god of the hedgehogs as much as of the humans; if there is not, well, the meaningless actions of sub-atomic particles affect us all equally too. Either way, we're all in this together and that, I hope you agree, is exciting. But you mustn't take my word (or anyone else's). *STA et considera miracula* – stop and consider the wondrous things and think it through for yourself.

THE GIGANTIC DRAMA

Vultures are seldom thought of as adventurous. We imagine them circling ominously or sitting in trees awaiting a death like potential legatees in an Agatha Christie. But fifty years ago, one daringly ventured seven miles up above the Earth. Unfortunately, we know this because a cruising airliner ploughed into it. It's still the highest-flying bird ever recorded – scant consolation perhaps. Almost as high, bar-headed geese soar over Tibet, looking down on the mountaineers who crawl up Everest to be on top of the world. Honk! Honk! Bacteria have been found higher still in the stratosphere, while down on the floors of the deepest ocean canyons, under the pressure of four thousand fathoms, snailfish and sea cucumbers pursue their mysterious vocations. Wherever we look on this planet, life is already there. 'What an infinity of infinities infinitely replicated, what a world, what a universe, apperceptible in whatever corpuscle one cares to choose,' cries the philosopher Leibniz, deliriously. There are even lichen living inside rocks; how do they manage that?

One day two billion years ago, a bacterium met an archaeon and merged, for the only time in history. Who (if there had been anyone around who could think at all) could have imagined that their heirs would spawn an elephant? or a record-breaking vulture? or all the multitudinous beings in the rainforest? There are more living cells than grains of sand. Not only is each of them unique, but every one is our cousin because we share one descent. In all this richness and abundance, we are, quite literally, one family.

It's a profligacy of existence we overlook, absorbed in self-reflection. Think of that famous icon of solitude, Caspar David Friedrich's painting *Wanderer Above a Sea of Fog*. Contemplative, maybe alienated, there he stands, high on a peak surveying the blankness of the foggy world below him. Apart from some distant trees and a spray of alpine flowers by his boot, all is lifeless. He is alone. Except... there will be tiny insects to pollinate those flowers, fungi between his weary toes, maybe even birds tweeting just out of frame. And microbes, of course. Lord, how many microbes! The human body aerosolises thirty-seven million microbes every hour. Speaking, farting, sneezing, scratching, we eject them into the atmosphere and breathe as many back in again. The Wanderer lives in a miasma of microbes, mobbed like the Beatles at an airport. And since these microbes are his cousins, every breath he takes is both a family reunion and a cannibal feast. Perhaps he has some inkling of this; perhaps that's what he's thinking about – a wonderer above a sea of fog.

We depend on this abundance. 'Why can organisms as disparate as humans and bacteria live together and co-operate?' asks the microbiologist Ed Yong. 'Because we share a common ancestor. We store information in DNA using the same coding system.' The affinity we have with the living world around us (which will be a theme of this book) is not whimsy; it is biology. We may not feel an emotional bond with *Streptococci* but already our bodies are working together without the need for our minds to get involved.

The Gigantic Drama

There is much more to the world than proud human isolation, much more to us than our thoughts. In fact, wherever we turn, there is much more.

This isn't the tone of most public discourse. Politicians want to narrow us down. They slough away nuance and complexity, valuing mindless support more than thoughtful questioning. Academics and journalists strive to 'explain' – to distil all the richness into a little file of words, but the richness doesn't exist to be explained. Words are not the reality that is waiting out there to be wondered at. The media crafts a little me-shaped doll and tries to persuade me that is what I am, so it can sell me stuff. And, as in some grim fairy tale, if I do not resist, I become that effigy. But I am, we are, more.

A walk in the woods, even a glance out of the window, reminds us. Nature is free of the blandishments of algorithms. 'Your feedback is important to us,' say half the emails in my inbox. Real things scorn such lies. This tree is not scintillating with autumn colour because it hopes that I might like it. Regardless of me, it's doing its own thing, discovering the world unmediated. As members of the family that's our simple privilege too – and there is so much to discover.

'Less is more,' say the design gurus. Nature, who never went to college, insists that more is more. It piles up possibilities. Do redwoods need to be so tall? Does a puffball need so many spores that if each of them germinated, one mushroom could cover the whole of Europe with a single puff? Do our minds need to be so wildly inventive? Must the kingfisher dazzle? Variety is the staple of life, not the spice. Creation, not survival, is its essence. We have foolishly decimated the world, and the less we are left with isn't more, but if we see nature for what it is and relish the ineffable fullness of it all, we can begin to love and care for it again.

So, look again at what we have left – it's still beyond comprehension. Of course we are astounded by the murmurations, the Northern Lights, the salmon's migration, but we need not rely on shots of awe. From the seabed to the stratosphere every cubic millimetre is occupied by creatures on the same mission of discovery as the tree. Thomas Traherne is even dazzled by dust: 'Some things are little on the outside and rough and common, but I remember the time when the dust of the streets were as precious as Gold to my infant eyes, and now they are more precious to the eye of reason.' He knows that wonder is not a luxury or a leisure-time activity; it is the element through which we see our ramifying world. All we need to do is stop and look. We can walk through the world each day as though it were a film we've never seen, uncertain what might happen next, alert to each new scene and mood in this gigantic drama. It may be the only live screening in the universe; it'd be a crime to miss it.

IN SEARCH OF SELF-EVIDENT TRUTHS

"We hold these truths to be self-evident, that all men are created equal, that they are endowed by their Creator with certain unalienable Rights, that among these are Life, Liberty and the pursuit of Happiness."

Self-evident truths. In drafting the Declaration of Independence, Thomas Jefferson was trying to build America's future on the surest foundation possible. But his claim that God ordained our civil polity no longer seems quite so self-evident. Such is the fate of all cultural ideas. They are temporary, local expedients. Aztecs, Vikings, Tibetan yak-herders and essay-writers in Radnorshire – we are each brought up with different notions about the world. To insist one group's traditions are 'better' than the others is only going to cause arguments.

So, where can we find some agreement? Perhaps we could set aside those cultural preconceptions and raise a world-view on a bedrock foundation of nature – the physical actuality that underpins everyone's experience? I call this simple plan 'STA' from the Biblical quotation *Sta et considera miracula* 'Stand still and consider the wondrous things' because a short and unfamiliar word carries least baggage.

STA makes only two assumptions – firstly, that the world is real and not some figment of your, my or anyone else's imagination; secondly, that evolution as proved by Charles Darwin is true. The outrage caused by *On The Origin of Species* had nothing to do with Natural Selection or any notion that the book denied the existence of God. The shock was Common Ancestry, Darwin's proof that all living organisms were descended from a single cell and were therefore all related, that there was no clear distinction between humans and the rest of nature, that Tennyson, Disraeli and even Queen Victoria were descended from monkeys. This was not what anyone wanted to hear. So, being deeply practical Victorians, they ignored it.

Two or three generations later, Bertrand Russell paused for a moment in his *History of Western Philosophy* to point out this continuing anomaly. He noted that anyone who believes in Darwinian evolution 'will find himself forced to regard apes as the equals of human beings. And why stop with apes? I do not see how he is to resist an argument in favour of Votes for Oysters'. Russell was content to make the joke and forget about it. Society has followed suit. We venerate Darwin for his great discovery and ignore its implications.

Instead, we are anthropocentric, believing that humans form a discrete, coherent species, separate from and superior to the rest of nature. All political and social ideologies are entirely anthropocentric, all religions have some tinge of it, as does much scientific research. Nature, however, is not.

So, STA rejects anthropocentrism, accepts Common Ancestry, takes a deep breath, stands still and considers the wondrous things around us. As it does so, these startling conclusions emerge:

1. Nature is real and the basis of our lives.
2. We are wholly involved in it and not separate in any way.
3. We generally ignore this affinity with nature, focussing on our own inventions (e.g., shopping, politics, football, TV etc) but …
4. … a rewarding sense of belonging is available to us if we accept it.
5. Nature unceasingly creates new, unique individuals.
6. Nature is perfect, by definition; its only purpose being to do whatever it does (though this, of course, may not suit our personal interests).
7. As each thing is unique, all things must be equal; individuality-with-interdependence is the basis of relationships in nature.

(The way these seven ideas first arrived in my head is described in Do Not Call the Tortoise. The arguments for each of them are elaborated in detail at sta-serial.com)

Now, suppose I take a STA-gazing walk up into the hills. Suddenly I can see that beneath my impressions of a picturesque landscape, a leisure resource, or a sheep-run, is something much older and deeper: this is *reality*. It is what *is*, and it is so with an unmitigated necessity. The world is not contingent on my thoughts; they are contingent on the solid reality around me – these hills, these hordes of innumerable creatures, all, as we have seen, my cousins – the thorn, the gorse and skylarks, horses, horseflies and these tiny yellow fungi – here, now, co-existing, co-habiting, co-creating this world with me. We experience the same conditions, subject to the same cosmic forces, busy at that same titanic task of 'endeavouring to persist in our own being', as Baruch Spinoza phrased it. I am not a *Homo sapiens* with 'exceptional' intelligence (that's for sure); I am a piece of nature coursing through nature, unceasingly and inevitably involved with everything around me.

This is a lost world rediscovered. STA peels away the coating of ordinariness in which we have shrink-wrapped our lives and reveals the pungent extraordinariness of reality beneath. These places I have known for years suddenly seen anew, the beliefs which have governed everything I do exposed as propaganda, these animals and plants around me already aware of it all.

> *Seest thou the little winged fly, smaller than a grain of sand?*
> *It has a heart like Me; a brain open to heaven and hell.*
> *Withinside wondrous & expressive; its gates are not closed.*
> *I hope thine are not.* (William Blake, *Milton*)

STA may be little known in Oxbridge colleges or Silicon Valley, but it's long been common practice in the hills and in the forests (and, of course, in cities too; it is no pastoral fantasy). Worms, warthogs and walruses don't theorise or conceptualise. They are alert to the weather, food and danger, looking for signals that it might be time for sex, vibrantly alive to their local reality. By the same simple process of paying heed to where we are, we can unlearn our human-centredness and reforge our broken links with the miracles around us. In every sense of the phrase, we can 'know our place'. We are not an isolated species; we are one of the creatures on the hill. We belong here too.

O! the one Life within us and abroad
(Coleridge)

Albeit less resonant than Jefferson's Declaration, STA is (or hopes to be) a modern rediscovery of self-evident truths to critique our errors and waymark our path. Clearly it has social, even political, implications – in a completely inter-related world everything ramifies forever – but it begins locally, not with grand ideas but with the solid facts, right here on this hill, all part of one unbroken reality, which underlies everything we think and know. Our interdependence reminds us of the vastness of the context in which we live; our uniqueness tells us, rather shockingly, that we are once-in-eternity beings. How magnificent and insignificant we simultaneously are!

Jefferson's self-evident truths helped overthrow an empire and proclaimed more hopeful values. STA may be less seismic geopolitically, but it's a startling shift in our everyday thinking. The world is not the thing we've been told it was. If we look afresh, we meet it more truly and humbly, and who can tell where that might lead? 'It is characteristic of complex systems that small actions can make a disproportionate impact,' writes the entrepreneur Margaret Heffernan. 'You just don't know, won't know, until you try'.

For me, this has been a vitalising, even transformative discovery: the reassurance of thoughts rooted in a deeper order than ideas and institutions; the alertness impelled by an ever-shifting world of uniquenesses; the liberty to act on my own experience – just like any other creature – without awaiting 'authority' from peer pressure or the media; the affinity and belonging in a seamless creation.

STA is a very simple idea, but that does not mean that its consequences are straightforward. In an infinitely complex world, it informs but cannot prescribe our actions, which remain our own responsibility. It is a beginning, not a resolution. That is the glorious burden of self-conscious existence – we are forced to be alert, and alive to the world. 'Through focussed attention the gift of truth is open to everyone,' Simone Weil assures us. We reconnect directly with *how things are* – that stone! that daffodil!! that person!!! – concepts, institutions, even words set aside. No longer puppets of fashion or habit, no longer fodder for mass media to graze upon, we have our own exhilarating freedom. *STA et considera* – Stop, look and think.

STA†E
T†CON
SIDER
A†MIR
ACULA

SIX TREES

1. Walnut – Home

The morning after the gales subsided, its long, hanging branches were swaying slightly, as though the tree were absent-mindedly humming to itself. My bed is placed so that the window frames it high above the scrub and the disused, low stone pigsties of the old vicarage across the road. A beech wrapped in a gauze of fine twiggery emphasises the walnut's gnarliness where every stub and knuckle is stark against the sky. Whatever dreams I may have had, whatever hopes and anxieties may be stirring, I wake to the unknowable but adamant presence of this tree.

Its limbs were wafting like seaweed in the tide, so I thought about air. We don't often think about air, until a storm stirs it into our attention. There is no empty space between myself and that tree but a dense and gently seething mass of air molecules as palpable as the sea (or for that matter the walnut) and that air must be speckled with midges, flies and floating micro-spiders (though perhaps fewer than in summer when swifts scythe across my view, snapping them out of the sky). A world in which I live and move and have my being hardly noticing a thing, mistaking invisibility for nothingness. And what would life be if the air were not invisible? A world without colour, barely with sight. 'I take it as a great kindness on nature's part to come into view every day,'

Ronald Blythe remarks. I will spend the day appreciating the air (and, of course, breathing it).

Last week, before the storm stripped the leaves, I woke to a calm day and the tree completely still except, within its mantle of motionless foliage, a single leaf high up pirouetting and flouncing on the end of its twig as though performing a solo dance to an audience rapt in silence. It often happens, at various times of year. Is it a micro-tornado or the work of some muscular spider or wasp? That's another thing I don't know.

MR BUN AND THE LEAVES AND FLOWERS

Once, when I was very small, I had a friend called Mr Bun. We were inseparable; we chattered away. Then one day he disappeared. It would have been heart-breaking if he had been real, but he was only an idea, an imaginary friend, and when my mind had no further need of him, he ceased to exist, and I didn't even notice.

Lots of children have imaginary friends or make up characters for their teddies and dolls. As we get older, we elaborate, like the Bronte children with their fictional worlds of Glass Town, Angria and Gondal. Eventually, people start calling us 'adults', but the fantasies don't stop. 'When I was a child, I spake as a child, I understood as a child, I thought as a child: but when I became a man, I put away childish things.' Well, if he's not just fibbing, St Paul is in the minority. We keep on making things up, and we can't always tell what's real and what's invented.

While other creatures respond exclusively to the facts of the world around them, we adopt the daring course of inhabiting our own inventions. We are the only life-form capable of ignoring reality – and we do.

To help navigate these hazardous cross-currents, STA draws a distinction between Necessary and Attributed Reality – the things that are definitely real, and those which we only say are real. It's easiest to explain with this example: the Sun and the river Amazon have a *necessary reality*. They exist whether and whatever we think of them. If we all close our eyes and pretend they don't exist it doesn't make a blind bit of difference – the Sun still shines, the river flows. They do not rely on our acknowledgement. The newspaper *The Sun* and Amazon.com, by contrast, have only an *attributed reality*. They have a physical existence – in fact, we can hardly avoid their shouty headlines and smiley brown packages, but if we all refused to recognise them, they would soon disappear like countless rags and retailers before them. Like Mr Bun, their reality is based on ideas and depends on our consent.

Once you can see them, it's amazing how many attributed realities you find. Parliament, institutions of any kind, classes, species, families, money, marketing, nations, numbers, business, property, even language itself – none has any necessary reality, but we make them the cornerstones of our lives. ('Imagine there's no countries,' sang John Lennon. I don't pretend to be first on the scene.) I have heard wry atheists find it laughable that religious folk invent a God, build a little house for him, and then ask him how they should live. But it's exactly what they and the rest of us do too. We may not know whether God is real, but we can be damn sure that the United Kingdom, the IMF and the Labour Party are not – we know we made them up ourselves.

Back in the real world, every organism is unique, and each is related to every other. There is me, and there is the whole world's biota; there is you, and there is the world's biota. All intermediate distinctions – nations, races, football supporters' clubs – are only made-up categories. Nature has no categories: no Israel or Palestine, no Hutu or Tutsi, no swallow or swift – they're all just fantasies. Species, as Darwin himself admitted, are 'artificial combinations made for convenience'.

Although attributed realities can be useful – that's why they were invented – none is a sure foundation; indeed our misplaced trust in them causes countless tragedies. There would be no war between nations without the fantasy of nations – Burgundy, Bohemia, The Kingdom of The Two Sicilies, 'Disneyland, Narnia, former Yugoslavia'. There would be no racial hatred without the fantasy of race, no anthropocentrism without the fantasy of species, and we know what the fantasy of money has done. The news is almost exclusively reported in terms of attributed realities. STA suggests a different approach, steadily rebuilding our worldview out of things that actually exist. It's a measure of where we are that this should seem at all odd.

It's not a new idea: Coleridge is on board already but, like John Lennon ('You may say I'm a dreamer') isn't sure that it'll catch on:

To Nature

It may indeed be fantasy when I
Essay to draw from all created things
Deep, heartfelt, inward joy that closely clings;
And trace in leaves and flowers that round me lie
Lessons of love and earnest piety.
So let it be; and if the wide world rings
In mock of this belief, it brings
Nor fear, nor grief, nor vain perplexity.

> *So will I build my altar in the fields,*
> *And the blue sky my fretted dome shall be,*
> *And the sweet fragrance that the wild flower yields*
> *Shall be the incense I will yield to Thee,*
> *Thee only God! and thou shalt not despise*
> *Even me, the priest of this poor sacrifice.*

Coleridge has always been passionate about politics – science, philosophy, theology too. Now, nearing fifty, he is as steeped in learning as anyone in history, but ultimately he rests his faith not in ideas but in the 'leaves and flowers that round me lie,' the necessary things.

Glance at the sun.
See the moon and stars.
Gaze at the beauty
of earth's greenings.
Now, think.

(Hildegard of Bingen)

JE †PU
IS †DO
NC †JE
†SUIS

SIX TREES

2. Banana Tree – Edo (now Tokyo)

In 1680, a poet called Tosei moved into his new home. Friends gave him banana trees to plant in the garden. He had been unhappy for many years, perhaps dismayed by the hedonism of the 'floating world' of Edo. He studied Zen Buddhism for a while and spent much of the rest of his life on the move, but he loved the banana trees.

'The tree has flowers but, unlike other flowers, there's nothing gay about them. The trunk is unharmed by the axe, because it's useless as timber for building, but I love it for its very uselessness ... I sit beneath it and relish the wind and rain that blow against it.'

Is there any greater honour you can pay a creature – banana tree, bird or person – than to treat it as itself, without expectation or prejudice, with neither sentimentality nor cold 'scientific' neutrality, with a sympathy that doesn't presume understanding? 'Maybe that's what love is,' writes the biographer Phyllis Rose, 'the refusal to see other people in terms of power.' We don't have to understand to love, but we cannot come near to understanding a living creature without such love. The poet loved the tree so much he renamed himself after it – Bashō.

RAISING GHOSTS

Robert MacFarlane, Katherine Rundell and Elif Shafak are three of my favourite contemporary authors. No shock there – they're critically acclaimed, bestselling prize-winners. All write beautifully, thoughtfully, inventively; all are politically engaged. I read everything they write, so why is it not enough to trust them?

Well, to be clear, it's not their fault. I doubt there are many writers alive I'd trust much more but every reader must 'doubt wisely', as Rundell's hero John Donne would say. Reading is a creative act: we bring our own experience to the text and so make something unique of it each time. If our attention is distracted the book stops dead, patiently waiting for us to begin again – it doesn't scroll on unregarded like music or the cinema. Reading fiction, we suspend our disbelief, but we do not expunge it completely. If the tale doesn't convince us, we give up. In history or science, though we cannot be expected to challenge the data, we keep alert to the way it is used, the historian's partiality, the excitable geneticist claiming rather more than the evidence warrants. Reader and writer collaborate, and the author who thinks the audience is only there to applaud had better beware.

But there's another reason to be wary too. We're all so close, all alive at the same time, living not far apart, digesting the same media, often following each other on Instagram. When some tragedy erupts in the Middle East, we see the same reports. When something happens in, say, Chad, we hear nothing at all. Our understanding is episodic and reactive. There is a conformity of contemporaneity beneath the surface squabbles of party and identity. Then peer pressure and the snug validation of likes on social media slide us into a rut of repetition, retweeting the cadences of outrage familiarity will mute. Algorithms offer complacency, confirming us in our views, which slowly cinch in, our arguments more predictable, our imaginations narrower. All huddled together in one culture-space, we stare at the world through the same window – and it's not a 360 view.

My three heroes know this. They break new ground. MacFarlane has reinvigorated landscape writing: in exploring mountains, paths and the underland, he is never restricted by boundaries and conventions. Rundell writes with a larkiness that vaporises cliché. She is steeped in Renaissance literature and sets each novel somewhere new with an electron's volatility. Shafak takes a fig-tree's or a raindrop's perspective and confidently runs concurrent plots in different countries thousands of years apart. They range over miles and millennia, but always bringing their wild explorations back to their purpose in the present.

> *Gathering all things in, twining each bruised stem*
> *to the swaying trellis of the dance*

For the same reason, this book is peppered with quotes, like that one from David Jones, and studded with inscriptions. Foreign tongues from foreign times, speaking to our situation without the tired tropes of our habitual chatter. Friends sometimes feel uneasy that I quote de Caussade or Traherne. They don't know who they are and suspect I'm showing off. Well, it isn't showing off and you don't need to know anything about those authors. The point, as with any art, is the work not the biography. *Caelesti sumus omnes semine oriundi – We are all born from the same celestial seed.* That's clear enough. It's the opinion of Lucretius two thousand years ago. It's a view, albeit poetically phrased, that Darwin and the Big Bang have confirmed for us, so we ought to take it seriously. But since our society refuses to do so, I'm gamely trying something different, enriching modern scientific fact with ancient classical wisdom.

These varied voices confirm our ideas as different co-ordinates fix a point by triangulation. There is also, I'll confess, a companionability. The world-view that STA propounds is so radically different from what appears on our news-stands that it's comforting to hear the friendly voices of this cloud of supportive witnesses. Books exist, among other reasons, to remind us we're not alone. As James Baldwin wrote, 'You think your pain and your heartbreak are unprecedented in the history of the world, but then you read.'

For most of human history, we revered (at times, unquestioningly) the wisdom of previous generations. Aristotle, Plutarch, Chaucer and Browne are thick with quotations. But from the seventeenth century, emboldened by science and new technology, 'enlightened' Europeans began to rely on self-cranked ingenuity, rejecting the past for their belief in a sunlit future of progress. After that fantasy of unstoppable improvement crashed so disastrously in the trenches of World War One – the new tech only murdering more ruthlessly, the ancient dream of human flight realised in a nightmare of bombing raids – TS Eliot bleakly tried to resuscitate the older tradition, shattered though it was. He filled his poem *The Waste Land* with debris salvaged from dead civilisations. 'These fragments I have shored against my ruin.'

All living things have always existed in a continuum without temporal or spatial divisions. If we are to address the problems that fill the news, we need, like Eliot, a much wider perspective than the news can give us. The past is not irrelevant because its people are dead; other cultures are not irrelevant because they don't speak English, other species are not irrelevant because they don't have self-consciousness and air-fryers.

There is an abundance of hard-won wisdom all around us. Robin Wall Kimmerer entreats us to learn from the gift economy of plants, so radically different from the economy of the stock exchange. Even in this room, there is the experience of cat, spider, woodlice, dust-mites, each finding its own trusted way to 'persist in its own being'. Four billion years of evolution have given us some breadth. *Uno itinere non potest pervenire ad tam grande secretum*, says an old Roman orator called Symmachus. *You cannot arrive at so great a secret by one path only.*

The inscriptions in this book show that STA's ideas have long been known. They are not some whims of mine, nor do they come from some brief moment called 'the past' which we oppose to our more important 'present'. They are cultural *miracula* spread over millennia: from Job in the 6th century BCE, it was five centuries before Lucretius, five centuries more to Symmachus, 700 years to the Sarum Rite, 600 to de Caussade and another two centuries to Simone Weil a hundred years ago – a consistency of wisdom undisturbed by the tics and spasms of news sensations.

All of us live in the here and now – the here and now of nature – but that batsqueak of nowness contains a good dollop of 'thenness'. We bear the experience of our ancestors in our genes; we are shaped by the wealth of our cultural inheritance and carry in our minds our own memories. Living in sync with nature demands an involvement of the past. 'We could never have loved the earth so well if we had had no childhood in it, if it were not the earth where the same flowers come up again every spring that we used to gather with our tiny fingers as we sat lisping to ourselves on the grass,' says Maggie in *The Mill on the Floss*.

MacFarlane discovers the old Tibetan word *shul*, 'a mark that remains after that which has made it has passed by'. Footprints are *shul*, paths are *shul*, all these voices are *shul*. Other people with different perspectives have been this way before. They offer multiplicity to our cinched world; the zeitgeist isn't the only option. Yuval Noah Harari believes this is the value of studying history, not to address specific issues, because our situations are always unique, but to learn from the changeability of the past that the future can be altered too. Nothing is pre-destined, and in a world which is infinitely varied and unpredictable, we may find openness, inclusivity and enrichment more helpful than separation and analysis. Our hope should be to understand better, rather than to know more.

The acme of elaboration is Renaissance polyphony, and nothing is more complex, more moving or more beautiful than Thomas Tallis's motet *Spem in alium*. Eight choirs, each of five voices, are arranged in an octagon around the audience. Each of the forty singers sings the same text but has a separate part. It is the epitome of the individuality and unity that all life on Earth displays. I am too ignorant of music to write at length. I can only marvel at the beauty of sound and philosophical perfection, and earnestly recommend you hear it and even, perhaps, follow the score, where the intricacy of its 'mystical mathematics' is, in part, revealed. *Spem in alium nunquam habui praeter in te – I have never put my hope in any other but thee*. Tallis, and the Sarum Rite from which the text is taken, are of course referring to God. I borrow the words for my trust in the whole created world of physical reality (which may quite possibly be the same thing, or a part of it. Who knows?)

The difference of each part doesn't undermine the unity, because the unity is already innate in them all; the unity of the whole doesn't compromise the individuality of each voice. There is never unison, no imposed conformity: 'One Law for the Lion and the Ox is Oppression,' thunders Blake, and the same applies to alto and bass. Instead, as the tramp in Tolstoy's *Resurrection* explains, 'Let everyone be 'imself, and us'll all be one'.

DOD DOD
YN YN
ÔL ÔL
AT AT
FY FY
NGH NGH
OED OED

SIX TREES

3. ARBOR

This is not a tree at all. It's an acronym; worse, it's a mnemonic acronym, the sort of monstrosity that belongs in corporate seminars, among FOMO-haunted wannabes. STA (not an acronym) is a reality-based world-view, and IRL there are no acronyms. So, this needs an explanation.

Well, it came serendipitously, as things do – the initial letters of a sentence I'd just written suddenly rising off the page like flares, and it has proved so useful and so easily memorable that I've steeled myself to share it. ARBOR (the Latin word for 'tree'): **A**cknowledge **R**eality, **B**eauty, **O**therness, **R**elatedness in every creature we meet – hedgehog, hedge-fund manager or tree. Each is unique, a once-in-eternity being, and therefore beautiful. Each is othered by genetic happenstance but part of our same great family and moved by our same needs.

There's a Welsh saying *Dod yn ôl at fy nghoed* 'going back to my trees' which means 'to return to sanity, to a balanced mind'. Trees are monumentally sane. A tree does not have a linear mentality, each day moving further from its origin away into the unknown; its world-view is cyclical. It grows by circling round itself, using its enfolded experience to negotiate the future.

I am too steeped in Westernism to feel those elemental cycles, but up in the hills, working in the garden or even just sitting in cafes I can ARBOR the creatures I meet: the hares and bracken, slugs and roses, friends and strangers, buzzards, beetles, baristas and curlews. I can acknowledge the reality, beauty, otherness and relatedness deep inside them all, and that's a return to the clarity and sanity of the trees.

LICHEN

Every New Year's Day or thereabouts I go to see the lichen at Llanbadarn-y-Garreg. Summer concealed them with thickets of bracken, but here again are the reds and whites and unexpected blues, the constellated dots as though some ancient ancestor had plotted the heavens on the sheer dark rocks. There are puffs of crimson or yellow dust on the walls – it hardly seems possible these are living beings. Little changes from one January to the next; the photos look identical. Lichen can grow a millimetre a year, but these, I suspect, aren't in quite such a rush. Entirely satisfied with all they have done, they resolve, this New Year, to do it again. They're disinclined to novelty.

My peppy eagerness to drive ten miles, clamber about and take their pictures feels mildly ridiculous in the face of such sagacity, and anyway the graveyard opposite my home is itself a lichen safari park, where the dead, weathering into anonymity, are graciously commemorated with living medallions, rosettes and epaulettes. Off-white, primrose and celadon are the muted tones of the honours here, but Ada Lloyd d.1910 has been granted a golden spray like a meteor shower – I wonder what singled her out.

Lichen are not single creatures but alliances of algae, fungi, bacteria and yeasts who patiently refute our heresies of competition and reductivism by enjoying a richness in partnership none could possess alone. Gently they erase the epitaphs, offering instead the gospel of example – quietude, smallness, endurance, togetherness and beauty.

UNIFIED LIVES

Introducing *Pandaemonium*, his extraordinary documentary account of the Industrial Revolution, the author and film-maker Humphrey Jennings wrote, 'At a certain period in human development the means of vision and the means of production were intimately connected or were felt to be by the people concerned – I refer to the Magical systems under which it was not possible to plow the ground without a prayer, to eat without a blessing, to hunt an animal without a magic formula.'

We have learnt a lot since those days: we know that the prayers and formulae of that 'Magical' society didn't really improve the fertility of the soil or the likely success of the hunt. But perhaps that was never the point. We flick a switch and a light comes on, we turn a key and the engine starts – cause and effect are tightly bound together in our mechanical world. But in the natural world where ritual began the fuses are longer, trailing out of sight and tangling into inextricable mare's-nests of complexity. The ploughman was not a dealer, trading a prayer for a bushel of grain. Instead, his prayer was (or began as) a spontaneous effusion, as natural as birdsong. 'O God I hope the seeds come up, otherwise we'll starve!' Over hundreds of generations, however, the rituals became more codified, diverging further and further from earthy reality until at last in our empirical age, they fell out of use, shamed as backward and irrelevant.

But the ancient rituals spoke to something deeper than

empiricism. The ploughman's prayer acknowledged his reliance on a power outside himself, with an unpresuming awareness of the world which is a pre-condition for taking care of it. In this more indirect way, that prayer *did* improve the soil's fertility. As all religions know, repeated behaviour reinforces belief. And that is how, in our own time, the daily ritual of heating a ready-meal while watching the news confirms our estrangement from the world, even at the moment we think we are engaging with it. The land, the food, the animals – we no longer have any relationship with them except that of consumer. We have voted to leave the community which the rest of creation continues to enjoy, and our habits deepen the divide.

That old 'Magical' system was vanishing from Europe even before the Industrial Revolution and was certainly extinct when Jennings was writing in the 1940s. Superstition had been eradicated, but so had our sense of affinity; one kind of ignorance had been expunged, to be replaced with another. Great gains had been won, but there were perhaps unnecessary losses too – above all, the sense of a unified life and world.

On a trip to Burma at this time, Jennings felt he may have glimpsed a culture which retained that unity long gone from the atomised West, a Buddhist society where every action 'from the weaving of the basket in which men carried their vegetables to market, to the burial of the dead, was … informed by a sublime metaphysical vision'. Perhaps it was so or perhaps he was just eager to romanticise the Orient, but either way the unity he sought, which was the same unity of that ancient 'Magical' society, continues to be practised, right under our very noses, by every other creature in the world – daisy, earwig, birch-tree, buffalo. For them, what they are and what they do are never in conflict; in fact, they are synonymous. Means and ends are inseparable. The thing at the heart of their lives is being themselves. This apple-tree is. It is what it is and is never distracted. It goes on 'is-ing' 24/7. It concentrates with pure intensity on being what, where and when it is. Whether growing or shedding leaves, flowering or fruiting, it follows its clear single vision. This fullness of being is the state in which all creation exists.

We, however, do things differently. We have unwittingly built ourselves a disintegrative culture. We lead fissile lives.

Imagine a man setting out for the office in the morning. He might, if pressed, say that the most important value at the heart of his life was his love for his partner and children. But active caring, or even the feeling of love, play little part in what he actually does. Instead, his entire day is spent in competition – with other commuters, rival firms, sometimes with colleagues, a series of low-level, barely-felt antagonisms founded on nothing but the conventions of business. The attempt to outdo someone is at the heart of all his actions (and he'd probably get sacked if it wasn't). Without even noticing he leads a self-contradictory life. The values he holds dearest – what he most deeply believes himself to be – and what he does all day have almost no connection. Means and ends are poles apart (and this may be stressful and mentally harmful). He might protest: 'Well that's how it is. It's a dog-eat-dog world.

The law of the jungle.' But dogs do not eat dogs; that isn't how it is. And the law of the jungle is about more than competition – it embraces interdependence, collaboration, symbiosis too. If it were merely a competitive environment, the strongest would make it a monoculture; but nature produces no monocultures – they are human impositions.

We are more complex than a daisy or a buffalo, of course. We have a dazzling variety of opportunities, but we need not be confused by them so long as our thoughts and actions grow out of a clear vision of ourselves and our place in the world. It's only unity of vision that distinguishes a palace from a builder's yard.

'The thing at the heart of their lives is being themselves.' This is what STA calls 'haecceity', or 'thisness' (pronouncing it 'heeks-ity' because the OED says that's ok, and because the other versions I've heard sound ridiculous.)

There is a quiet particularity in each of us that is ours and no one else's. How to describe it – a flavour? a language? a voice? a dog would say 'a scent!' It is made of everything we are – our anatomy and physiology, abilities and perspective, the experiences and memories which constantly re-mould it, because it is never static but tremulously sensitive to circumstance. It's more profound and comprehensive than our ego or personality, those purely psychological elements which easily become self-conscious,, and it's not something reducible to DNA. It's the whole complexity arising out of all these elements combined, the us-ness of each of us.

We needn't boast, because every moth, every stickleback and liverwort has it too – uniqueness is a condition of existence – but it is, I think, something to be cherished, the delicately personal slant on the world which colours everything we do. Perhaps we should pause from time to time to pay quiet homage to our haecceities, as the Ancient Greeks would celebrate their *idios daemon* or inner spirit.

Haecceity implies the O, the otherness of ARBOR. Since each of us is unique, we cannot claim to know another person; we cannot know ourselves because we are in constant flux and our data is already out of date. We must tread gently, at ease with our mystery; to define ourselves (or anything else) is censorship. Identity groups based on gender, nationality, sexuality, offer welcome community, but can only ever reflect the tiniest fraction of what we are, which is more complex, more confusing, more exciting. Each of us has multitudinous identities, which is why I prefer the term 'haecceity.'

We live hidden in plain sight, but our ignorance of our selves is only a microcosm of our general unknowingness. An ease with the smaller may accustom us to the larger and keep us from over-confident blunderings. Most of the tragedies that fill the news began in over-confident blunderings.

So, if I stand a moment in the garden and exercise my haecceity in looking round me: here is this fennel, here at this moment, in this light and this breeze, seen by me from this angle with these no longer very young eyes and this brain packed with memories sparking volleys of ideas (perhaps of delicacy, aniseed, food; perhaps fragility, climate change, death; who knows where the mind will run?), but for now, here is this fennel, and it and the moment and my response together comprise a fragment of the universe exclusively revealed to me. This is *le sacrement du moment présent*. If you were beside me, your angle of view, your different eyes and preoccupations would generate something slightly different. (The fennel meanwhile has its own less verbose experience of our encounter.)

This practice of looking – seeing what is, seeing myself seeing it, knowing the intermixture of all living things – settles us in our surroundings, like a hare half-hidden in its form. Our haecceity gives us a subtly independent vision. When we are told what is expected of 'people like us', we are already primed with an anticipation of difference. Scepticism is too negative a word; haecceity is not a pose of contrariness. It's rather the precious self-reliance shown by any plant or animal which never surrenders its agency.

Business, institutions and the media – the forces that control public life – hate haecceity. They speak in an ultra-processed language of generalisations and demographics. They standardize, simplify and algorithmify us into ten thousand made-up categories – customers, voters, minorities, target groups, GenX, GenZ, classes and races, erecting barriers between us and, of course, dividing us from the rest of nature. Sometimes they try to commodify haecceity, claiming we can satisfy our wild particularity by wearing their mass-produced lipstick or driving their mass-produced cars. Mostly they deny it, using the power of their ubiquity to persuade us that theirs in the normal view, with which we should comply. It is obviously reasonable for politicians and bureaucrats governing a nation of millions to use some of these macro-abstractions. But it is crucial that we are not beguiled by the media line that the macro is the truest view of life, that demographics can be scaled down on to individuals, that statistics mean anything. These are fantasies no other creature would credit, and that humans have only recently been fooled into believing.

How do we protect our haecceity from the grinding expectations of conformity? It isn't always easy, as our conflicted commuter could testify. 'It actually takes a daily effort to be free,' writes Geoff Dyer. Poetry and novels can help. Both are attuned to 'moments of being' and individual characters with their own internal worlds. (I recently re-read Virginia Woolf's *Mrs Dalloway*, every paragraph written with microscopic sensitivity, every character linked to the others.) But the surest way is alertness to the solid certainties which surround us – bird, tree, person, or this plantain finding a chink in the kerb with an urgent lust for existence. 'Stand still and consider the wondrous things.' The rewards are certainly generous. Because we are unique in every moment, no blueprint dictates how we must behave. When we refuse the rule of stats and demographics, haecceity puts us back in charge of our lives with no guarantees, until death. As Gillian Rose wrote in *Paradiso*, we 'venture again the courage of suspense, not knowing who we are, in order to rediscover our infinite capacity for self-creation and response to our fellow self-creators.' We meet the world naked and free; being who we are becomes our greatest adventure.

Haecceity was first identified by the medieval scholar Duns Scotus. Reading him six centuries later, the Victorian poet Gerard Manley Hopkins was thrilled to realise that he could put away the abstract theories of his theological training and find meaning, even God, through this world of solid things.

> *As kingfishers catch fire, dragonflies draw flame;*
> *As tumbled over rim in roundy wells*
> *Stones ring; like each tucked string tells, each hung bell's*
> *Bow swung finds tongue to fling out broad its name;*
> *Each mortal thing does one thing and the same:*
> *Deals out that being indoors each one dwells;*
> *Selves — goes itself; myself it speaks and spells,*
> *Crying 'What I do is me: for that I came'.*

'For that I came', not to conform or acquiesce, but to bear irreplicable witness to the world.

THE INSCRUTABILITY OF WOODLICE

Gustave Flaubert didn't think much of woodlice. Of *Madame Bovary*, the novel in which he exposed the smallnesses and hypocrisies of French provincial life, he wrote 'All I wanted to do was render a grey colour, the mouldy colour of a woodlouse's existence.' This smacks of prejudice.

Some months ago, I spent an evening watching a woodlouse. It came quite boldly through the drawing-room door, not skirting the wainscot but advancing across open carpet towards the sofa where I lay. It ignored the stacks of books on the floor, reached the sofa and began to climb. When it reached the top, it turned to follow the ridge along the back before descending the other arm and heading for the hearth. The fireplace surround is fifteen bricks high – again it climbed. The higher it went, the more slowly it went until on the twelfth brick disaster struck and it fell. But miraculously only three inches down it clung (or perhaps I should say was caught) by one leg on the rough surface of the brickwork. There it hung for almost half a minute. Eventually it righted itself and, propelled by ambition, stubbornness, misinformed hunger or who knows what, continued the ascent. On the mantel as on the sofa, it walked along the ridge before taking some time to consider its return. Understandably after its fall it was wary of the sheer descent down the brick face, but it seemed similarly mistrustful of the smooth paint on the wall. After a few false starts it opted, like a seasoned climber finding a 'chimney', for the angle between them – left legs on the brickwork, right legs on the wall – and so carefully reached the hearth again at which point I toasted its achievement and went to bed exhausted by the drama.

What its achievement *was*, what a woodlouse can achieve from its own perspective, I have no idea. It didn't eat anything or have any sex, which we might rather snootily have assumed constitute the sum of woodlouse existence, but nor, I imagine, could we say it was compelled by a spirit of adventure. All we can suggest is that its own life is in few ways as 'mouldy grey' as Flaubert believed bourgeois, hypocritical human society in mid-nineteenth century France to be. Its interiority is a deep, dark mystery to us. For all our knowledge, I suspect we understand little more of a woodlouse's existence than it understands of ours.

Weeks later, again on the sofa, (*Recumbe et considera miracula – Lie down and consider the wondrous things*) surrounded by the usual detritus, I noticed another woodlouse sauntering across the open pages of *Hamlet*. (I say 'another', but it could have been the same indefatigable explorer. I'm not an oniscideologist.) It didn't pause to read, of course. What did it make of this summit of human achievement? Well, I suppose it saw the marks on the page, maybe felt the indentations, but had no conception of what they meant, or that they meant anything, or that there was such a thing as meaning. Still, within the limits of its own, woodlouse view, *The Complete Works of William Shakespeare: The Cambridge Text* must have been quite comprehensible: it was a thing to be walked across as, differently textured, were the carpet, newspaper and plate. Can we claim much more? When I walk across the hills, is their latent meaning as wasted on me as *Hamlet* on an arthropod?

SPEM†

IN†TE   IN†AL

AETER   IUM†N

UI†PR   UNQUA

M†HAB

SIX TREES

4. Oak – Oxfordshire

A trip to the capital passes through a verdant idyll of sluggish rivers, gentle hills, lonely churches and startled deer. We halt at Honeybourne, Charlbury, Kingham, places that probably do not exist.

Uncrowded trains are good places to work. Once, bemused by my scatter of notebooks, I jotted in one, 'I don't want to write a bloody novel, I want to write.....' and the sentence was left as blank as my mind until a stately oak alone in its pasture among those mythic villages glided into view '..... a tree'.

How do you write a tree? I don't know. But the essence of a tree is ramification, ceaseless changefulness, stretching out, reaching down into the ground with unimaginable intimacy. A tree absorbs the world around it – the air, the light, the water, the minerals. It grows by inclusion, transmutation and division, giving out oxygen, shelter and food. Even after death it ramifies in the life it gives to the fungi, microbes, insects that destroy it, the birds and animals that feed on them, the whole business going on and on, but no longer labelled 'tree'. And that is also the business of books. They absorb, transmute, penetrate and feed.

Children's literature is best at this. *The Phantom Tollbooth* and *The Mouse and His Child* don't repeat information but gradually show that what you thought on page 1 may no longer be adequate. 'Look at the strangeness,' they say. 'Just look!' They give what Russell Hoban called an 'onwith', the found meanings they discharge like the tree's waste oxygen, which ramify in the reader long after the final page.

PHLO FLOW

WHAT DO I WANT?
   TO SPEND MORE TIME WITH PHLO
   ALL ELSE FLOWS FROM THAT

This appeared in my notebook one morning.

I remembered: I woke in the night, reached for a pen, scribbled this in the dark and went back to sleep. I'd been working nonstop for weeks, was worn out and wanted to be at home with my cat. Nothing odd about that. Phlo and I have lived together for 6 or 7 years, and I can say without blanching that we love each other deeply. We are not so co-dependent that we have no other joys: she retains ancient instincts for hunting shrews and snoozing under bushes (less so when it's raining); I have more acculturated habits – books, Shiraz, ancient movies – but 'All else flows from that'? What was that about? It seems more than 'have a nice rest and you'll feel better' – the sort of useful if banal judgement my rational brain might make. 'All else flows from that': a thought so urgent that it startled me awake, so mysteriously important I wrote it in capitals aslant a page of more careful ruminations – this is an irruption of deeper feeling like a sinkhole opening in a suburban lawn. What did it mean?

It is in these eructations of thought, these belching-forths from the unknown, that buried connections are revealed. This will not be an 'I love my cat' essay; why should I bother you with that?

It is, more unusually and with hair-raising ambition, a 'my cat is a portal to the universe' essay. And if mine is, so is yours. 'All else flows from that' as my sleeping self observed.

Here is Phlo, purring patiently on my lap. How, beautiful as she is, can she be a portal which connects me to everything? How can my sleeping instincts be justified?

Here is the scientific answer:
– all matter in the universe was once concentrated into a singularity from which it burst thirteen billion years ago

The atoms which are currently Phlo have been biffing about the universe ever since. Recently they had the good fortune to become her, but they won't be detained for long. Some of them were tuna a few hours ago; others will soon be in the litter tray. The atoms themselves are gloriously pluralist, indifferent to their host: fish, Phlo, cat turd, animate or inanimate. Would that we were all so easy-going!

– all living things are descended from a common ancestor.

We know this from evolution. If you had half of eternity, a piece of paper the size of the galaxy and nothing better to do, you could draw up a family tree with Phlo somewhere near the bottom (though how many zillions of creatures have been born in her lifetime?) and trace the link between her and that buttercup, her and Nijinsky (the dancer or the horse), her and the tuna she ate for her lunch – but I'm sure you have something better to do.

– everything we do ramifies with infinitesimal consequences for ever.

The Butterfly Effect (where a butterfly flapping its wings may, among other factors, 'cause' a tornado on the other side of the world) is a famous example of this, but more melodramatic than our purposes require. The basic point is the minute but eternal, if unpredictable, influence on our environment. Nothing is lost. When we toss a pebble into a pond the ripples never cease.

Here is the mythological answer, described by Timothy Brook:

'When Indra fashioned the world, he made it as a web, and at every knot in that web is tied a pearl. Everything that exists or has existed, every idea that can be thought about, every datum that is true – every dharma, in the language of Indian philosophy – is a pearl in Indra's net. Not only is every pearl tied to every other pearl by virtue of the web on which they hang, but on the surface of every pearl is reflected every other jewel in the net. Everything that exists in Indra's web implies all else that exists.'

This is a magical image of the interdependence of everything that is. It shows an exquisitely balanced, infinitely complex, sufficient and sustaining universe. It is perfection and needs nothing from us but wonder. Modern science and ancient lore converge. Phlo is a pearl, and in her I can see everything.

This is not sentimental guff about pussycats. I suppose a cactus or an armadillo in my lap could equally remind me of those scientific facts, or I could contemplate a carrot or a toadstool, but it's better with Phlo. Emotion can enhance truth (as well as sometimes obscure it) – we have riches deeper than reason. Phlo personalizes all the grand abstractions, realising science in love. There are times when I get hassled or frustrated, and she reflects my mood with fractious miaows. I pick her up and cuddle her not merely to reassure her or for the warmth and comfort she gives, but because she is so unmistakably real that all the worries of work, gossip, rudeness or parking fines are unmasked as petty mind-trash.

Here I sit (as Luther almost said). From this armchair, I am connected to everything. All else flows from that. Such a stillness and freedom from social fretting this gives, a defusing of expectation and ambition, a centredness, a reassurance. Here. Now. It's OK. I don't need to be anywhere else; I'm not missing out unless I ignore what's in front of me. This is how Phlo assesses the world – not with theories, divinities or stories but with the world of sense and experience that connects everything that is, starting here. Your lowly hedgehog knows the world this way too.

We don't need to begin with the microscopic or the macro, with quantum mechanics or cosmology, with genes or populations. The world exists at multiple levels, and this cat-and-bloke-in-armchair level is as real and valid as any. [Footnote: I'm sorry to include a footnote, but this may look like empty braggadocio without some evidence to back it, so to be technical: the biologist Michel Morange explains, 'Biological function emerges from the complex organization that scans the whole scale of life, from microbes up to whole organisms, or even groups of organisms.' 'Each level has its own rules ... All are essential; none can claim priority,' adds Philip Ball. So, here is as good a place to start as any. We are not just the consequence of sub-atomic or genetic actions, nor are we wholly determined by our environment. As we're already thick with quotes, here's Karl Marx, 'Men make their own history, but ... they do not make it under circumstances chosen by themselves.' This is important because it confirms our agency, albeit in context, which otherwise gets gnawed away by advertising, expectation, habit etc. For Simone Weil, it is this precious agency that makes us what we are: '*Je puis, donc je suis.*' '*I can, therefore I am.*'] We are always at the centre of this polycentric universe. Here is this cat. I don't have to move. She doesn't tell me school facts – equations and laws and such like – and she doesn't *explain* the universe to me – she's a cat and, like the rest of nature, has never bothered with explanation. Is it useful to her to know why it rains, or why a pile of books nudged off the table hits the floor so satisfyingly? Well, I'm more interested in that than she is but frankly I've never found it *useful* either. But the true relationship between myself and every other organism – the belonging, the affinity, the scale of the context in which I live and my uniqueness within it – which I have finally discovered so late in life, would have been as valuable every day as I find it now. I wish I'd learnt that in school.

*   *   *

I wrote a rough version of all the above a year ago and then left it as I became busy with other things. Free again, I was planning to revise it when Phlo suddenly died, a painful decline from sprightliness to hopelessness in a week. We loved each other as I've said.

STA is generally a beautiful, celebratory way of thinking, but its focus on physical reality can, at times, seem harsh and grittily unsentimental. It offers truth rather than consolation and there are times, I'll admit, none more so than bereavement, when consolation would be more welcome. But it's a philosophy with a solid bottom of stoicism, based on looking at what is and taking that as the basis of one's relationship with the world. No dreams of afterlives, no invented concepts like money or nations or ideologies, no wishfulness except those hopes that we by our efforts might achieve ourselves. Just a grasp of the sufficiency of everything that is. As Rilke sternly puts it, 'Whatever is, is right.'

So, much as I'd like there to be, there's no cause for complaint. The death of someone you love is something the world does and so it's something you take. You don't stop loving, you cherish the memory (and I'm phrasing this in general terms for obvious reasons). The butterfly fluttering at the window is just as miraculous as it was before, even though its vitality seems like a calculated insult, and you would willingly sacrifice every butterfly in the world if it would bring your loved one back. But that's meaningless, Laertes-like posturing. She's dead. We die. The world wouldn't work if we didn't. And till then we live, and that butterfly *is* beautiful and so, bless it, is the spider whose web it has narrowly dodged, and so it goes on. Miracle after miracle wearing away the resentment and, more slowly, the grief. And when I open the window to let it out, there's the whole damn tapestry of miracles – sparrows and cotoneaster, dogs and dog-walkers; the carnival goes on around the corpse. Nature doesn't cancel the performance out of respect. That's how it is – the indelicacy of reality. I can either accommodate myself to it or disappear into a fantasy world, and given the irresistible is-ness of reality – there goes that butterfly! – there is only one possible path.

* * *

And now, five months later, here is Cyrus, sweet and shy, better by far than a cactus or armadillo. A portal to the universe? Yes, but incidentally so; first and foremost, she's herself. As I try to revise this ramshackle essay, Cyrus sits immovably on the pages with a wry assurance of her necessary reality, and the mere contingency of the words beneath her bum. [Footnote: I hadn't meant to get another feline companion but the discovery of a rat in my wardrobe decided it. My passionate love of all creation does not involve wanting it all in my bedroom. That the best suited creature at the Cats Protection League should already have the same name as the imprint under which these books are published is very odd indeed but, surely, a meaningless coincidence.]

U
NO
ITIN
ERE ✠ NON
POTEST ✠ PER
VENIRE ✠ AD ✠ TAM
GRANDE ✠ SECRETUM
TAM ✠ AD ✠ PERVEN
IRE ✠ POTEST
NON ✠ ITI
NERE
UN
O

SIX TREES

5. Liquidambar – Y Fenni/Abergavenny

In the sliver of suburb between the station and the town stands an incandescent liquidambar like a candle flame. It's a shock in the soft November light.

I've always been attracted by the idea that autumn leaves disclose their real colours, latent all summer beneath the dominant green until the chlorophyll ebbs as the days shorten. I like that looking-glass-world unexpectedness, but I've learnt that it's not completely true. The truth is still more topsy-turvy.

The liquidambar is not red and gold. The summer leaves were not green. They appeared so because green is the colour in the spectrum the leaves cannot absorb, and which is reflected back at us. It's like me eating a pizza but leaving the anchovies on the side of the plate. I am in a very real sense dough and mozzarella, mushroom, olive and onion – these are being absorbed into my body, vegetable metamorphosing into animal, but I am not anchovy. As I reject the fish, the tree won't swallow green. It is violet indigo blue ... yellow orange and red – everything but green. (So I suppose my hair is all the colours of the spectrum except grey – I'm beginning to like this idea.)

Does this mean the world is capricious and that we cannot trust our senses? No, simply that we judge too quickly what they tell us. And since what goes for the colour of leaves, goes for people too....

NOT MRS TIGGYWINKLE

Warning: contains mild exasperation

'Hedgehogs are the UK's Favourite Mammal with more Google searches and Instagram hashtags than any other animal.' They were voted Britain's National Species in a BBC poll, and the UK's Favourite Mammal in the Royal Society of Biology's public vote with more than twice the votes of the second-placed fox! Oh, we LOVE hedgehogs!!! ♥ ♥ ♥ ♥ ♥

But hedgehogs are also on the Red List of Endangered Species, their numbers in freefall, their survival chances somewhere between unlikely and zilch.

There is plainly something of a contradiction between what we say and do.

We vote in online polls, and we go into our gardens to count birds and butterflies for 'important national surveys'; we do all these things that the media ask of us, so why isn't nature thriving? The answer is crushingly simple: because we don't stop flying, or driving needlessly, because we buy tat and throw it away, because we grub out hedges, disinfect, spray, pollute and kill. Because we sponsor businesses, industries and governments who do all this on a much grander scale. Because voting in online polls is worthless, because responding to marketing never ends well, because there is a REAL world and there is a made-up world, and we have temporarily lost our capacity for telling which is which.

It's not as though we haven't been warned. Forty years ago, the great David Attenborough closed the last episode of *The Living Planet* with these words: 'Clearly, we could devastate the world... Its continued survival now rests in our hands.' Billions of people have watched that film, and the devastation has accelerated. He couldn't have been plainer or more eloquent: why has he not persuaded us? Perhaps the problem lies in the medium, one in which warnings of global catastrophe are quickly followed by Pets on Ice, Celebrity Origami and people pretending to be serial killers for our evening's entertainment. Perhaps there is a category difference between watching TV and meaningful action.

The disjunction between our hopes and our behaviour is so blatant (we love hedgehogs, and we kill them all), perhaps it is enough to expose the basic problem: our actions are piecemeal and short-term, disconnected from each other and from any guiding principle. We live without a coherent world-view.

We are seldom as evil as our deeds might suggest. We do not kill hedgehogs because we hate their snuffly ways; loggers felling rainforest in Brazil or Malaysia are not intoxicated with some weird sap-lust. We don't mean to do much harm. But cock-up is as costly as conspiracy. Clever tech fixes and economic bribes may mitigate the problems but, so long as our mental attitude remains bored, self-indulgent and lazily acquisitive, they are unlikely to suffice.

STA offers a coherent world-view, based on reality rather than ideas or fantasy. It says that our chief business in life is interacting with the real things around us – water, trees, people and, of course, hedgehogs. Not a cartoon, not Mrs Tiggywinkle, but a flea-ridden, flesh and blood creature striving like us, though even more precariously, to exist in a growingly hostile environment. STA meets the world at eye-level and loves it so much it takes it seriously.

Try it. Set aside preconceptions, think about those seven starting-points (listed on page 19), disentangle the necessary from the attributed realities and ARBOR them. Be still and consider the wondrous things. Whoever we are, wherever we come from, if we start from that bedrock foundation, rather than customs or trends or peer pressure, we can be sure of our footing and commence whatever activism (or quietism) we think fit. Although each of us is unique, if we begin together from the same sure place, I doubt we'll drift too far apart.

STA is pretty robust. In fact, I can't see how you can dispute it once you accept that the world is real and evolution true, but if you think you find some inconsistencies or there's something else you can't stand in these pages, there are other options to explore. Only, whether your choice be Buddhist or Jain or pagan or animist or Shinto or one of the strands of an institutionalised religion like St Francis's Christianity, it must accept our rootedness in a complex, interdependent, animate world, showing respect for all life, an admission of our own innate limitations and alertness to the consequences of our deeds. We've learnt enough to know that anything else would be dishonest. Buddhism and those other belief-systems are different from STA, but they overlap, and it's not a competition. All, anyway, wonder at hedgehogs and leave them alone, rather than idolising, hashtagging and exterminating them, and so they're surely saner than you're used to.

Five hundred years ago, a Welsh poet imagined a squirrel going to London to protest at the felling of her oak wood, Coed Marchan. She complains to the Council that she has been left homeless, that the owls are cold, the wildcats bewildered, and the goats and pigs left with nowhere to forage. '*Yn iach draenog*'*. It's not as though we haven't been told.

* *Goodbye hedgehog*

75

† MOMENT † PRÉSENT † LE † SACREMENT † DU †

SIX TREES

6. Plane – near Sardis

Not much is certain – the evidence is sketchy: a line or two in Herodotus, some later comments on that. It was two and a half thousand years ago. On his expedition to destroy the Greeks, the Persian emperor Xerxes halted his million strong army, the largest ever assembled, and kept it kicking its heels for a day because he 'came across a plane-tree of such beauty that he was moved to decorate it with golden ornaments and to appoint a guardian for it in perpetuity'.

Who knows what he saw? Some glimpse of the ineffable? An oasis of shade on a long, hot march? A fine specimen to interest an arborist? It was autumn when he passed that way to Sardis. Perhaps it was simply loveliness – the changing leaves, the mottled bark, the scraps of sky in the opening canopy – a kaleidoscope of beauty startling a mind bent on slaughter.

Historians have ridiculed him ever since; they've sniggered that he 'fell in love'. What good was jewellery to a tree? But that's a rational objection, and praise is not a calculation. It has no more 'purpose' than the pumping of our blood. (Our hearts don't beat 'to keep us alive'; we're alive because they beat.)

Xerxes wanted to rule the world; gold and dreams of eternity were his currency. I love plane trees too; I take some photos, maybe write a little essay. We each make our offerings as best we can, some sort of acknowledgement of something.

Later, when a storm destroyed his ships, he had the sea flogged and fettered, so perhaps he was crazy after all. The evidence is sketchy – not much is certain.

Post script
In *Pilgrim at Tinker Creek*, Annie Dillard also reflects on this story. I mention this as an excuse to recommend it yet again. It's a wild, astonishing book, ever new.

BACON & KEATS

A child said 'What is the grass?' Fetching it to me with full hands, How could I answer the child? I do not know what it is any more than he.
                                    (Walt Whitman, *Song of Myself*)

What is the grass?

There are two different paths to understanding which flow uneasily alongside each other like the M4 and the Thames. You might call them active and passive, perhaps even sense and sensibility. I'll call them Bacon and Keats. One is pragmatic and fashions reality to suit its own ambitions, the other more humbly adjusts its own life to harmonise. For some time now, the former has been the much busier, noisier route. All the heavy freight goes that way, bustling with acquisition and accumulation, following Sir Francis Bacon's dictum that 'knowledge is power'. It's an insatiable, capitalist approach to learning. There is always more to know, to possess, to control; there will always be greener grass than the stuff the kid brought. There's no rest for the Baconians. It exhausts them and everything around them.

Each of us is in a life-long relationship with the world. Imagine going out with someone who started running background checks on you – blood group, bank balance, known associates – trying to find out as much as possible to gain the upper hand. That is not how relationships are supposed to work. There needs to be love, trust, space, appreciation of each other's mystery. The weirdos who want power over their partners should be investigated by the police; the same applies to our relationship with the world.

Fortunately, this isn't the only option. The ancient stream still flows alongside the gridlocked motorway. This book began with the unknowability of a tree and the gaggle of humans staring up at it. I've spent as much time in the subsequent pages reminding you I don't know things as telling you anything I do know. Unknowability is like an aura enveloping each object and each creature in the world, revealing them as ever-new, beautiful, richer and stranger than we thought, and worth our rapt attention. John Keats knew it as 'Negative Capability, that is, when a man is capable of being in uncertainties, mysteries, doubt, without any irritable reaching after fact and reason' – without Google or ID apps either. It is an unfenced paradise where we are free to roam, blooming with wild questions no fool has dug up and re-potted as answers; no names, no categories, no complacent pretence of knowledge, but an older, quieter route to understanding – by engagement and affinity. He watches a sparrow picking around in the gravel outside his window and 'takes part in its existence ... nothing startles me beyond the moment.' Not a critic or spectator like the shrewd Baconians, but part of the great drama.

What is the grass?
Science formulates and pins down what it can. It heaps up facts but doesn't answer the question, indeed complains it is meaningless.

The more fascinating discoveries science makes the more surely the unknowability is revealed. The identification of the littlest particles, the sequencing of the genome have given us no ultimate answers, only vanishing horizons of complexity. Perhaps it is time at last to put away the notion of 'answers', summits of knowledge to be conquered like Everest. ('Honk honk!' laugh the bar-headed geese.) Common sense tells us plainly enough that in an ever-changing world of uniquenesses, everything must finally be inexpressible, since language works by comparing things to other things and so denying their uniqueness. It is a tool to help us get by, not the key to Omniscience. Your lowly hedgehog knows the grass like the woodlouse knew my Shakespeare – enough for its own needs. If any god is a god of the hedgehogs as much as the humans, that's presumably good enough. The universe does not require our clever explanations, just our taking part.

> Erfüll davon dein Herz, so gross es ist,
> Und wenn du ganz in dem Gefühle selig bist,
> Nenn es dann, wie du willst:
> Nenns Glück! Herz! Liebe! Gott!
> Ich habe keinen Namen
> Dafür! Gefühl ist alles;
> Name ist Schall unt Rauch,
> Umnebelnd Himmelsglut.

> *Fill your heart full of this, big as it is,*
> *And when the feeling inside you is complete delight,*

> *Call it what you like:*
> *Call it Happiness! Heart! Love! God!*
> *I have no name for it!*
> *Feeling is everything –*
> *The name's just sound and smoke,*
> *Clouding the light of heaven.*

>   Goethe, *Faust (trans. David Luke)*

But what about our brilliant complexity? Do we have to 'dumb down' to a hedgehog's intellect? Well, we could certainly emulate its disdain for ambition – the rest of creation would be very relieved – but no. The ancient riverine way does not deny our genius but redirects it in the service of honesty rather than wealth or power. All over the world, we have found ways of expressing ourselves without self-assertion or destructiveness, straining every synapse to say, '*O altitudo! – How fathomlessly wonderful!*'. In ancient India, there was the *brahmodya*, a competitive debate to define the ultimate reality, the *brahman*, which always ended in silence at the impossibility of the task. In the medieval Greek Orthodox church, Karen Armstrong tells us, any statement about God had to be 'paradoxical, to remind us that the divine cannot fit into our limited human categories, and apophatic, leading us to silence'. Tallis's *Spem in alium* follows that path, displaying all our astonishing, ever-ramifying talents, bringing everything we have to lay on Coleridge's 'altar in the fields' and retreating, abashed that even such richness is inadequate. This is the jewel of philosophy, the triumph of wisdom over intelligence. *STA et considera miracula* – not because by thought we might wrangle our way towards an absolute truth, but because by standing still, being there and considering we may be as close to enacting one as we're likely to get. Our task is to be ourselves, not to achieve control, not, perhaps, to achieve anything.

In the Ashmolean is an ancient stone carved with mysterious lettering. Does it tell a tale of heroes? Or of an emperor's bloody conquests? Is it just a dreary docket of goods received? Although it proclaims its message to thousands of visitors every week, no one has a clue what it says. No one can read Eteocypriot script. I put its pic on Instagram #unknowability. My phone told me the hashtag had been used fewer than 100 times. A quick wildly random search revealed that #wggrace, a long dead cricketer, had over 1000, #liztruss, the most unsuccessful prime minister in history (a competitive field) over 30k, #chocolatecake 16 million, #taylorswift rather more. #unknowability seems off the pace. Perhaps that is appropriate. Will society ever recognise the depth and beauty of unknowability? You never know.

LIFE IS CREATIVITY

I don't suppose this will ever happen, but if some wealthy and indulgent friend offered to show me any piece of art anywhere in the world, I'd ask to see Lascaux, Chauvet or Altamira where our ancestors twenty, thirty thousand years ago filled caves miles deep with astonishing paintings of horses, aurochs, bison, bears and the other great beasts of the Ice Age.

There is a primal creativity about these images – direct and irreducible to the terms of modern art-world chatter. The work is not simply the marks on display as with a Rembrandt or Picasso which can hang as well in New York or Amsterdam, but the marks where they are as part of where they are and what they are only because of where they are, just as a tree or a stone takes its form from its environment. Art and place are mutually integrated; context is everything.

The predators paint the prey. These are not the efforts of a special caste of stay-at-home 'creatives' but people who knew the animals' anatomies because they lived by chasing, killing, butchering them. They knew lions as Titian, for example, did not. Their lives are integrated too. These were not cartoon cavemen; born into our culture they would assimilate as easily as our siblings.

The question we all ask is 'Why did they do it?' and we answer according to the academic fashions of our day. Since Altamira was discovered in the 1880s, the various theories have been: to create beauty in a dark and dangerous place, to teach each other the best ways and times to hunt, 'for ritual purposes' to achieve success in the hunt, to appease the spirits of the creatures they must kill, to express their awareness of the inter-permeability of the physical and spiritual worlds, to say, 'I was here'.

Imagine asking of European artists since Giotto: Why did they do it? For God? To show each other the glory of God? Of the king, the state, the patron? To show off? To make money? To get good reviews? For the fun of it? To say, 'I was here'? Both societies are too complex, the periods too long, the work too varied for a single specific answer to suffice. If we still bicker about Carl Andre's pile of bricks and wonder what Antony Gormley means, we can't pretend to certainty about pre-historic art. Any 'answers' will certainly be unprovable, at best inadequate and quite possibly just wrong.

Instead, I want to suggest that, true or not, all of these guessed purposes are secondary and answer the question with this bold claim: *Because making things is what all living creatures do and have been doing for four billion years. In short, because life is creativity.*

Art is not a piece of cultural cleverness that separates us from the beasts; it's a natural process that we share with them. The first cell on Earth divided and made another cell. And so it went on – cells growing and dividing, plants making pollen and setting seed, spores, sperm, eggs and babies. The story of life is one of making. As organisms evolved and became more complex, this same drive to create showed itself in new ways. Our ability to perceive the world at all is an act of creativity. The images that form separately on my two retinas are combined and edited into 'what I see', just as surely as a painter selects and prioritises.

Virtus artis constitit in judicando, wrote Aquinas. 'The essence of art consists in selectivity.' While you're reading this, your fingers and thumbs feel the texture of the pages, perhaps your mouth has got a little dry, your ears have registered cars passing in the street – all this data has been couriered into your brain and your brain has sent it away. 'I'm busy; I'm reading this fascinating essay. Don't disturb me unless it's an emergency,' it says, at some level way below our consciousness.

Our deliberate cogitations follow this same inherent process. Every plan or idea is an artwork. What we think of as 'art' – the Sistine chapel, *Some Like It Hot*, *Aida* and *The Gruffalo* where thoughts, feeling, imagination, memory are fused and refashioned into physical form – is the same fundamental impulse in its most complex manifestation.

> *The Force that through the green fuse drives the flower*
> drives my pen across this page.

This continuing billions of years old history gives an awe-inspiring context to our work. This a world of creativity. As you begin to sketch that portrait, your reference is not simply the latest trends, nor even the history of Western portraiture from Ancient Egypt to Lucien Freud, but all life on Earth – a daunting but liberating discovery. Movements, isms, influences, egotism, the market fall away – you're involved in something much deeper and richer than that. As the literary critic Azar Nafisi explains, 'In all great fiction, regardless of subject, there is an affirmation of life ... The perfection and beauty of form rebels against the ugliness of subject-matter.' However anguished and doomy Munch or Bacon may appear, the very effort of their mark-making draws them into communion with the whole of creation as, at least subconsciously, they must have known, or they wouldn't have bothered. There can be no nihilistic art, because nihilism believes in nothingness and art keeps making somethings.

Ultimately, we create not because it is good for us, teaches us, forces us to be aware, unites the world and binds us to it, nor because it is fun, though it is all those things and more, but because it is our nature to create. As the flower processes the sunlight into nectar, we process the universe into art. It is as natural as that.

Lascaux is closed to the public now. The sudden irruption of visitors after undisturbed millennia changed the atmosphere; black mould creeps across the walls. In much the same way creativity has been obscured by the connotations we attach to it – a toy for the wealthy, a refuge for misfits; dangerous and subversive or irrelevant and effete – and the various corruptions of money, celebrity, bureaucracy and power. But art is an entirely normal and natural activity. No one is naturally a politician, a window-cleaner, solicitor or taxi-driver, but we are all naturally artists. 'I don't reckon the artist to be an extraordinary man,' says the painter, Cecil Collins. 'The artist is what's going on in everybody, but focussed to a point of intensity.' Art is metabolism: receiving an input and transforming it into an output. It is the most complex example of a process common to all life. But it is no less a privilege for being universal.

So, I can't go to Lascaux, Chauvet or Altamira, but I can look at the pictures in books and online and then put them away and imagine, and perhaps that's an appropriate tribute. They were not made to be scrutinised like Raphael's *School of Athens*, but glimpsed in flickering pine torch light, seeming to move as the flame guttered, the swells and clefts and concavities of the walls, stone animated as tender flesh, assuming new shapes as our wonderstruck ancestors moved around the cave. But while we can look at these images and whirl our minds around them, we can also make anew. We needn't fret about our lack of talent; we don't have to show our work to anybody else. The first value is in the doing. Many of the ancient cave paintings were tucked away in crevices where they would not be seen – the act of making was more important than the images produced, certainly more important than display (which may explain why many are over-painted). Nature creates; it is not interested in exhibitionism or our presumptuous aesthetics; it just makes and makes with dizzying profligacy, more and more and more. Taste is a cultural invention. Art, and all creativity, is natural before it is cultural. Making art (in whatever form) is the most complete expression of what we are, joining the stream of creativity which flows through all living things.

O altitudo!

THE INSCRIPTIONS

Caelesti sumus omnes semine oriundi – We are all born from the same celestial seed. Lucretius, 1st century BCE Roman philosopher poet.

Sta et considera miracula – Stand still and consider the wondrous things. Book of Job c.6th century BCE, in Latin Vulgate translation by St Jerome 4th century CE.

Je puis, donc je suis – I can, therefore I am. Simone Weil, 20th century French philosopher, activist, ascetic and extraordinary person.

Dod yn ôl at fy nghoed – going back to my trees. Traditional Welsh saying of unknown date.

Spem in alium nunquam habui praeter in te – I have never put my hope in any other but thee. The Sarum Rite, 11th century, used by Thomas Tallis in his motet c.1571.

Uno itinere non potest pervenire ad tam grande secretum – You cannot arrive at so great a secret by one path only. Symmachus, 4th century Roman statesman and orator.

A number of these are available as letterpress inscriptions on cards or postcards at sta-website.com

ACKNOWLEDGEMENTS

I am deeply indebted to Graeme Hobbs for designing and setting the text, for creating the beautiful, evolving inscriptions, for advice, patience and a gentle insistence on high standards. He is very good at standing still and considering, which is a rare accomplishment. Visit fallowpages.art for more of Graeme's letterpress work.

I'm hugely grateful too to Ella Sutton for the drawing of such a wise and welcoming hedgehog on the cover, as well as the leaf-snuffler on page 74, and for her enthusiasm and support for the whole project.

Hedgehog was born out of the unexpected success of its predecessor *Do Not Call the Tortoise*. Many thanks to all its readers, especially those who were so kind as to get in touch, and to the bookshops that gave it its chance.

Printed and bound by Orphans Press Ltd, Leominster/Llanllieni. I'm especially grateful to Martin Parry, Katie Shearer, Gary Nozedar and Debbie Hatfield for their expertise and helpfulness.

Printed in Garamond on Olin paper with Rives Tradition cover.

Published by The Cyrus Press in 2025
ISBN 978-1-0369-1052-5

www.sta-website.com

STA is a way of looking at the world rather than an intellectual and verbal argument. The website offers a visual alternative to the more literary approach of this book. It's unhurried, unexpected, playful & rather odd.

staetconsidera.substack.com   @considerthewondrous

CAELESTI

SUMUS

OMNES

SEMINE

ORIUNDI